Tools for a new trade

Finance, strategy and markets in the digitized economy

Dan Ramsden

New York, August 2016

Tools for a new trade

Copyright © 2016 by Dan Ramsden

All rights reserved.

ISBN-13: 978-1537088334
ISBN-10: 1537088335

D. Ramsden

Tools for a new trade

D. Ramsden

Preface

The basic premise: An industrial and consumer environment built upon ubiquitous connectivity, affordable and sophisticated computing, virtually unlimited data storage, and category convergences driven by the resulting information flows, will necessarily feature a different set of qualities (at every level) from those to which we had become accustomed in bygone times.

Tools for a new trade

The fourteen chapters of this book were originally published as a weekly series in the spring of 2016. These had isolate different aspects of the environment described, presenting them with an emphasis on finance, strategy, markets, valuation, and general economic issues impacting enterprise and individuals alike. The posts, mildly edited, are collected here as a unified essay because it actually is a whole, with a beginning and a middle, and an end.

This is not presented as a forecast but rather as a depiction of where things currently stand, as seen through a lens shaped by many years of use, informing an outlook that, so far, has proven reasonable. If the depiction bears resemblance to the actuality you see through your lens, too, then hopefully you will find your ideas articulated well. If your lens presents reality differently, then I hope you will nonetheless gain from a different perspective to enrich your own. The world that is presented here is in important ways unprecedented, and we all stand to benefit as one another's guides.

D. Ramsden

Tools for a new trade

D. Ramsden

Contents

1. **Introduction** – overview of digital dynamism and its transformations.

2. **Fundamentals** — the basic unit, the systems that form from it, and ingredients of their value.

3. **Methods** — businesses, plans and the spectrum of options in an unsteady domain.

4. **Comparables** — presence and attention as new reference points of competition.

5. **Expectations** — innovation, disruption and the consequence of high velocity that has become the norm.

6. **Leverage** — forms of debt that are not strictly financial and the new costs of such borrowing.

7. **Cycles** — reinvestment, reinvention, repackaging, with Apple as a case study.

8. **Markets** — the new climate and its moods, and the resulting focal points.

9. **Resources** — networks, optionality and gaps in our understanding of both.

10. **Term** — the expected life of products and the structures that they shape, with Facebook and Netflix as case studies.

11. **Diffusion** — effects of speed and limitlessness on Economics and its principles.

12. **Concentration** — emerging stores of value that are data banks, too deep to fail.

13. **Portfolio** — strategy and speculation during constant change, and the enterprise as a form of managed diversification.

D. Ramsden

14. **Specialization** — the individual, the changing world and our ceaseless preparation.

Tools for a new trade

D. Ramsden

1. Introduction

In the fall of 2013 I published another short collection called The Age of Convergence, to capture assorted aspects of what I perceived to be a new economic era emerging. The common thread running through its chapters was as follows:

- In an economy increasingly shaped by information processing and flows, digital technology is not merely a tool but the core business in fields as varied as finance, commerce, healthcare, transportation, entertainment, education, and even heavy industry. These sectors and others would increasingly overlap, pulled by a shared language of mechanized knowledge and the processing of its bits.

- The evolution is from an age of hyper-specialization to an era of synthesis and combination, and an emerging set of new fundamentals needs to be understood holistically. Elements that were previously apart are beginning to blend and unify, and we see this in pairings of design and logistics, content and distribution, networks and applications, hardware and software, products and services, and previously distinct areas of finance and capital flows.

- These massive global changes, which have happened at historically unprecedented speed, are driving a need for business and economic theory to adapt, as aspects of inflation and deflation, employment, productivity and growth, supply and demand, financial leverage and value, all take new forms, new meanings and new stature.

Since the publication of the book in 2013, evidence has continued to mount of the described environment taking hold, and what may have been a theoretical set of observations at the time has these three years later become immediate and increasingly real.

We have during this time seen Apple branch out into consumer finance and television (two examples among several), Amazon into everything from infrastructure to the connected home to entertainment production to freight, IBM into artificial intelligence served to every major sector, and Google into areas as seemingly remote as health. We note that Goldman Sachs is moving to redefine itself as a technology and data processing enterprise, while technology and data processing companies such as Uber and Airbnb are presenting themselves as global networks that enable vendors and consumers to intermingle and overlap. Venture capital firms like Andreessen Horowitz support portfolio companies with business services, while large and mature companies in virtually every industry are establishing venture initiatives, startup incubators and accelerators to provide financial and operating support to disrupters. Self-driving car technology is being pursued by startups, Uber, General Motors, Google, and Apple.

And all the while, the adoption of latest technologies has become standard behavior at all levels of the economy, as the pace of innovation is unabated — now in new areas of virtual and augmented reality, artificial intelligence, robotics, and blockchain applications.

An investigation, therefore, in recognition of such realities, seems now even more timely, if not urgent. Questions about economic policy or whether there is or is not a market bubble, for instance, are lacking in substance unless the current-world qualities described (and others) are factored in. The opportunity at every level is to (re)evaluate assets and direction in a modernized manner consistent with a new era, characterized by new fundamentals. In the process, some may discover and

Tools for a new trade

capitalize on inefficiencies that remain, or otherwise rectify these to create value.

In the next chapter the new fundamentals and systems will be introduced and analyzed.

D. Ramsden

Tools for a new trade

D. Ramsden

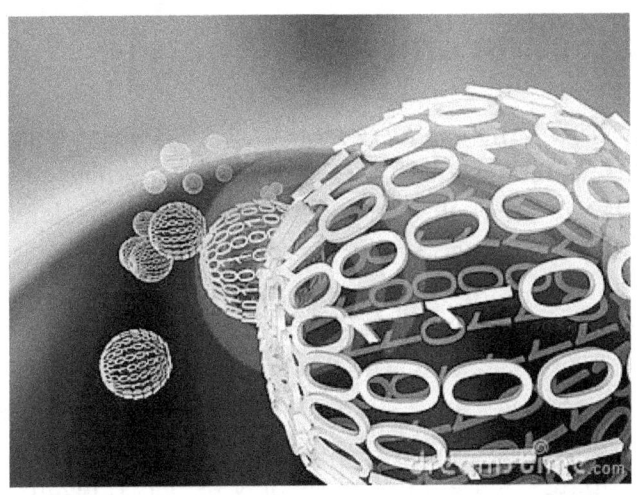

2.Fundamentals

Here, a general thesis is presented, a theoretical groundwork — beginning with the digital raw material and ending with the finished possibilities — before proceeding to particulars in the following entries.

The production unit and its nature

At the core there is the *production unit*, which is not the bit but what its batches stand for. We may generally call this *information*, although it includes a great deal besides and varies with the category. In the sense of media there is content. In finance, commerce, and industry there is data. There is knowledge more broadly in science, education, law, and so on; in all services. The list is extensive and its categories tend to overlap.

Information, as defined, is a fleeting substance when left alone: it dissipates, it's gone, it lives only as it is relevant. News and behavioral changes are information that might only be momentary. Some has a longer shelf life, such as, for instance, an editorial piece like this one, but the useful life of information is always at risk, even in the sciences. Supply and demand factor in and complicate calculations, and when dealing with information we are in a realm of perpetual supply, almost by definition. For purposes of this discussion about information that is shared in bits, we may conclude as follows: It is a transitory, replicable, non-scarce asset.

Systems and their economics

The unit is processed through systems. These serve to renew, replenish, refresh the life and thus the value of production, more or less effectively as different information lends itself to such processing more or less readily. Information systems in the technical sense of data bits and their flows have tended to be *deflationary* in nature. Moore's Law, open source, web distribution, shared storage, innovation and other continuous efficiencies of digital technology contribute to a lowering of barriers and business costs, and to individual and business consumption expectations predicated on "free" or, at the very least, an improved price-value dynamic over time.

In this environment of a slippery production unit processed through deflationary systems, enterprise is built to create sustainable value: no easy feat when bits are of essentially infinite supply and technology is tending to limitless accessibility. It does so, sometimes, in a variety of ways. These include areas such as technological upkeep and improvement, feature integration, economies of scale, security (and other defenses), brand presence, interactivity, network effect... That last item was left to the end of the list for emphasis, because it comprises aspects of the others and may be the most important. (A future installment in this series will be dedicated to it.)

Ingredients of value

A common thread, explicit or implied in the preceding sections, is the constant flux, the state of perpetual becoming, never quite arrived. This influences valuation in ways that are more pronounced these days, even if the notions are not new, because of the two-fold composition of enterprise value: an *asset* and its *optionality*. The former is the foundation, the actuality, and the latter is its future possibilities, many of which (if not most, maybe all), unknowable.

In a digital era when software is dominant, the risk of obsolescence is material and consumption patterns are quick to change. For an enterprise to preserve its asset and grow into its option value it must continuously fine-tune and reload its systems. In the financial sense, this raises questions about longevity and the future willingness of buyers, of its product and of itself... all of which questionable to varying degrees.

On a relative scale, the balance between asset and optionality varies with different types of enterprise and different stages in the enterprise life-cycle. At one extreme, for the startup the value proposition is mainly option based. At the other extreme, say, the mature utility, option value will be very low. In neither case is option value nil, nor is the asset unbreakable; which is to say, all businesses, even the most mature, have aspects of a venture now: a blend of actuality and possibility, each depending on the other for sustenance, all while deflationary systems continuously process a never-ending stream of fragile information units.

Consequences in finance

The presented thesis with its framework of bits and systems, and the resulting blend of assets and options, is what increasingly seems to shape capital flows in the digital economy. Funding structures, at least theoretically, are determined by optionality on the upside and asset coverage on the downside, as the expected life and value of the asset varies with its product, its platform, or its network, and the value of the option is enhanced by the same volatility that may cause the underlying asset to be disrupted.

The nuances of venture capital, later-stage lower-risk equity, debt funding in its many manifestations... the differences between liquid and illiquid positions... strategic versus purely financial investment... and the timing of acquisitions and exits, could all be revisited in this context. By the same token, questions about investment bubbles or bursts, if isolated from it, are prone to over-simplification.

Other consequences

According to observers, we migrated some time ago from an industrial era to one driven by *knowledge work*. To the extent that knowledge can now be mechanically reproduced, shared, or even improved, there may be reason to revisit economic subjects such as employment, inflation, productivity, and growth, from this new perspective (infinite supply of product, deflationary systems, the state of constant flux, etc.).

Although many businesses, or parts of businesses and industries, are not directly impacted by digital transformation, the trend is pointing in that direction. Financial value, and by extension money flows, is about what will be rather than what was, and so, perhaps, the discussion is pertinent regardless.

In the next segment, a look at new forms of enterprise that have emerged, predicated on the foregoing.

Tools for a new trade

D. Ramsden

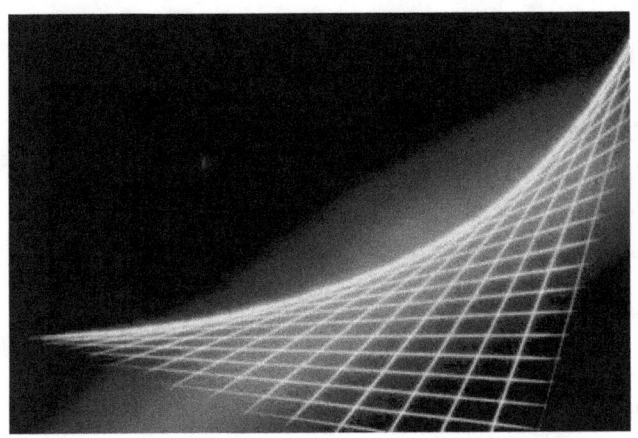

3. Methods

In the previous section, the subject of value drivers was introduced, particular to an economy centered around digital information systems. The relationship between the business asset and its optionality was noted at a theoretical level, when such systems are built on an infinite supply of bits in a deflationary software environment marked by constant change.

In the current installment the commentary is about more specific value and strategic considerations when foundations are fickle, and massively scalable, at once.

Tools for a new trade

Breakage of the constant

The discounted cash flow model and its derivatives in standard valuation metrics — the core of our financial conventions — have reinforced a way of thinking that is rooted in a distant and increasingly foreign era. This was a time when a car manufacturing plant or a retailer or a bank were reasonably expected to preserve their essence into the distant future, when growth was aided by varying degrees of inflation in a normalized economy, and when a plan was mainly predicated on what sort of expansion or contraction to assume.

As we find ourselves in economics rapidly transformed by digital technology and the mechanized processing of information, in a period characterized by ceaseless innovation and redefinition, such traditional qualities have been shaken up. Expected future value — which is a present value to someone in the future and the critical output of financial forecasts — has traditionally been based on a premise of continuity (or worse still, perpetuity), and is thus especially prone to breakage. The subject business may indeed grow or shrink but would leave us guessing nowadays as to its actual nature as the years pass by. The mystery is now not only about bigness or smallness, but even more basic: What actually will it be?

We used to reminisce about typewriters and pagers, but soon it will be printers and maybe desktop computers, hard-drives, scheduled television programs, distributed content in general, credit card transactions, point-of-sale terminals, retail shelves; then there is stock trading, driving, educating, manufacturing, one's office and home, all on their way to software reconfiguration, which leads to so many other things...

Reinvention as a business model

Although the form of enterprise and its substance are increasingly fluid, the analytic solution is not to discard the financial model or its components — and their connections to strategic planning, funding, or valuation metrics — because there is a logic to the age-old system that cannot be displaced. The idea, rather, is to recognize the new realities and the markers that they trace around all those interconnected things; and to apply qualifiers accordingly. In a framework of assets and options, for instance, (as was proposed in the prior post), businesses must continuously refine direction, and sometimes change course altogether, just to preserve (let alone grow) their value.

To illustrate, note current reinventions by IBM as an artificial intelligence platform and GE as a software company supporting an industrial internet; note the investment of capital and resources by Alphabet Inc. into healthcare and transportation, among other activities that are (superficially) unrelated to Google search; or note the experimentation on which Amazon prides itself, resulting in business lines such as Amazon Web Services (AWS), now dominant in the organization and really the sector worldwide. Most interestingly, perhaps, note the continuous activities of the big network itself, as Facebook keeps adding layers and dimensions of connectivity (Instagram, WhatsApp) and application (streaming video) and technology (virtual reality), never at rest (as a matter of principle) in what should be the comfortable "moat" of network effect.

The commonality is not only a refusal to take future value for granted, that goes without saying, but a refusal to accept the present form as something that is lasting.

The new formula

Seen through this lens, strategies and their evaluation may assume vastly different parameters. The analysis is complex (and generally still nascent, I believe), and conclusions seem to vary with differences in subject; but, nevertheless, several key observations are discernible and certain basic precepts have tended to jump out. Here is a handful of these, in a sort of order of associated ideas, that leads to a critical conclusion towards the end:

1. Along the spectrum of information-based enterprise, technology at one extreme comes with shorter life and higher disruption risk than networks at the other end, which are harder to break... (a) Many businesses fall in a zone between the polar ends, or combine elements of both that need to be considered on a blended basis... (b) The timing decision of investments is as important financially as the development of a new business line is strategically, and, by the same token, the exit strategy is critical for both... (c) The value of a product will quickly diminish unless upgraded or refreshed.

2. A focus on revenues and profits is strictly speaking necessary for a business that seeks to stay independent, but not all businesses seek that or should do so, even if some might pretend to for tactical reasons... (a) A flexible business model is not a bad thing for purposes of building optionality, but that can only be stretched so much before the

benefit no longer offsets disorientation likely to ensue... (b) Some businesses are good at making money, and some are not; the former is not necessarily superior to the latter, nor more valuable, but each may want to pursue the other as partner, depending.

3. Business strategy, based on the above, is increasingly like the management of a financial portfolio... (a) Option value is governed by rules of **convexity**, in which downside is limited in relation to the occasional positive outcome, which is outsized for the cost incurred... (b) The companies most likely to succeed long-term, and thus capture the greatest and most lasting value, are those with the wherewithal to keep up their portfolios and renew their option pools with regularity, the concentration of which will be reflected in a **power law** distribution.

Below are a few exemplary comments from Jeff Bezos, digital economy pioneer, to Amazon shareholders. They have done quite well.

> Most large organizations embrace the idea of invention, but are not willing to suffer the string of failed experiments necessary to get there. Outsized returns often come from betting against conventional wisdom, and conventional wisdom is usually right. Given a ten percent chance of a 100 times payoff, you should take that bet every time. But you're still going to be wrong nine times out of ten. We all know that if you swing for the fences, you're going to strike out a lot, but you're also going to hit some home runs. In business, every once in a while, when you step up to the plate, you can score 1,000 runs. This long-tailed distribution of returns is why it's important to be bold.

In the next chapter, the challenges of competitive comparison will be taken up, as directions have started to converge.

D. Ramsden

Tools for a new trade

D. Ramsden

4.Comparables

The transformations catalyzed by massive, rapid adoption of digital technology in every economic segment have been the central themes of the series, with emphasis on financial and valuation consequences. In this fourth segment the focus is on competitive analysis, as this reflects the same fast adoption and consequent big changes.

Tools for a new trade

Competition in a vacuum

As the peer group of a business matters to it when assessing its competitive positioning and formulating a plan, so it also matters to the financial analyst when estimating the value of the enterprise. In finance, the analyst typically extracts comparable ratios from a designated group of similar types, making adjustments for size or growth rate, and applying some appropriate range of results to the subject company's metrics. This can be done with current data, as a multiple of revenues or earnings for instance, or it can be applied to a future estimate in order to derive a future value. This is standard practice, and, as mentioned, may parallel strategic planning and competitive assessment in the enterprise itself.

When competition is evolving, reflecting perpetual changes in technology or the customer expectations that track such changes, the described comparisons, whether for strategic planning or financial evaluation, assume a more intricate texture. For example, it is not the case anymore that a retail operation can be quantified by changes in square footage and same-store sales and seasonal merchandise and so on, because now there are also issues of e-commerce and mobile applications and social media and Amazon, which, formerly a retailer, is now also an entertainment outlet with its eye on payment technologies, among other things. Thus, whether Amazon is more comparable to Walmart than to, say, Apple, or whether it is competitive with Google as an online commercial destination, is no longer a straightforward call for it, for Apple and Google, and increasingly less so for Walmart. The "field," in other words, is not zoned and fenced in anymore, and if it is, the fence is probably eroding.

They say that one should skate to where the puck will be, not where it is, but the hockey analogy falls apart when the puck is (or could be) everywhere and move in all directions. For reasons suggested, and because value is based on what will be rather than what is, the discussion is not merely theoretical or limited to the digital technology segment proper, in its current form. Our competitors are always around to meet us, we only must know who they are.

Attention and its reference points

In typical commentary about new technologies and platforms, language has served as a frame of reference for purposes of comparison within and between isolated segments. For instance, we call some of these *adtech,* or *fintech,* in advertising and finance, or we refer to *the cloud* and *SaaS* models and *mobile* applications, and we call some of these *bots* and refer to their connectivity as *networks*. But these are mainly software assets and the segments, as labeled, are flawed categories: There is overlap between them, and within each there are sub-segments that don't have as much in common with one another as a shared label implies.

For a more correct perspective, perhaps, we could instead revert back to basics and take in all these emerging areas of digital bits and systems through a lens of *supply and demand*. If we define the supply-side as, more or less, data (or, as was referenced broadly in the second installment here, "information"), this is, as was argued, infinite, or, if you prefer, vastly sizable and perpetually replenished from a seemingly endless trove. Demand, on the other hand, is much more limited because it is bounded by available time and capacity to process. We could think of the demand-side as *attention*, and although this may not be the perfect name it serves an important purpose in establishing perspective and parameters.

In an information economy, especially one centered around the mechanized flow of bits, competitors (or comparables) — whether today, in five years, or into implied "perpetuity" — are going to be those suppliers of product who fight for the same finite demand (i.e., the same attention). For purposes of current discussion about ways to categorize a given digital business and to understand its competition, there are some qualifying questions that further the thought process. Here is a sample:

- Whose *attention* does the business, or asset, or system seek?

- By what means does it do so, (and by what means preserve it)?

- Whose attention may be sought by it in the future using the same or similar means?

Even if segmentations are blurrier now and the contrasts not as sharp; even if attention is not necessarily associated with human consumption directly, but with another system along the supply chain of information flow; and even if supply and demand can be circular or reflexive in nature, one might still argue as follows:

The more similar a given subject is to another in the types of questions listed, the more comparable and thus the more competitive are the two.

Comparisons of Presence

The bigger comparables in traditional financial analysis have tended to be valued at a premium, reflecting the market influence that size can perpetuate. Bigness as a competitive edge has not diminished in significance, but the way we measure it and the way we think about its *likelihood to last* is different when digital assets are the subject. The bigger "comps" may not always be measured by revenues or assets, but could instead (or in addition) refer to the size of data sets, to the depth of systems, and to a *presence* in the gathering and distributing of bits: or, stated differently, a presence of market attention.

(The "winner take most" perspective that many in the venture capital community have adopted to measure a startup's potential is a manifestation of the *presence* concept here considered, and this is often predicated on *attention* rather than revenue or asset quantification. The rationale is not unsound: In the contest for attention in an economic system of plentiful digital supply, presence can sometimes breed demand in a circular fashion. Also implied in this way of seeing things is a general tendency to commoditization and deflationary economics, as has been considered in this series before and will again.)

A key distinction between the old and new economies, at the root of changes in comparison and competitive reference points described, is that the software core of the new enables its participants (with effort) to expand,

Tools for a new trade

contract, change form and seek to target different areas in new ways, at almost any time. This represents both opportunity and challenge in business building — the opportunity enhanced by presence and the challenge magnified by a never-ending contest for attention. In both cases, the threat of digital disruption is perpetually hovering, and altering one's perception of who is, or who may become, a competitor.

In the next piece the significance of disruption will be considered, when innovation is no longer a surprise, but is expected.

D. Ramsden

Tools for a new trade

5. Expectations

In previous chapters here it was suggested that the speed of recent technology-driven change (as much as its magnitude) has had a destabilizing effect — in industries and the broader economy — that was rooted in uneven recognition. As we now enter a period in which the changes and their pace have been absorbed (and in most circles, accepted), what may have been an initial disorientation seems to be subsiding, and uncertainty is giving way to a path that is in some aspects more predictable. But, while planning and investment decisions may be smoothed out as a result, expectations are being accordingly reset.

In this fifth episode of the series, a summary is presented of how we arrived to this point, and what it might mean for strategy, finance and valuation going forward.

Tools for a new trade

The turbulent ascent

Although the Internet and the industry that it created were popularized in the 1990s, one might say that the modern world of digital technology more truly emerged with the introduction of the smartphone — if a demarcation point has to be picked — a handheld supercomputer in billions of global pockets. Parallel advances in data gathering, processing, safekeeping, and distribution have created new systems and methods in virtually every field. Because it is easier, when making note of big changes, to point to big symbols, here is a sample of very big objects that were transformed or have repositioned in the period: Microsoft, GE, Ford, Dell, IBM, Verizon, Wall Street, banking, all communication, urban transport, hospitality, education, retail, entertainment, services, the workplace, the home...

With exceptions and explanation for individual circumstance, these transformations took place over much less than a decade, in certain instances just in the past few years, and the sums of capital involved or impacted are beyond estimate. Of the top-10 companies worldwide as measured by market capitalization, half are now in the core technology sector (including the top-3), and most of the others are on the fringes and moving in.

On the surface, *innovation* and, more to the point, *disruption* (which implies breakage and thus a volatile event), became operative words during this time. Beneath the labels, however, more substantive shifts in atmosphere were forming — as illustrated — that make the buzzwords seem almost trivial. There is something much more monumental and historically consequential about the environment that has emerged, something that seems far greater than mere economic cycle or technology evolution.

It feels like an era of its own, that one day will be looked back upon as a defining and redirecting period — such as the Industrial Revolution — and needs to be understood as such. The new atmosphere, arrived at in no time at all, has changed everything.

At cruising altitude

With an event of change, the novelty itself does not necessarily trigger instability; the principal actor, rather, is the velocity of the change (or the sharpness of the contrast). By the same token, when change is happening continuously, what may lead to some imbalance is acceleration or deceleration (increase or decrease in velocity). Now that the velocity of innovation seems stable (albeit, at a high rate), now that transformations are happening at a steady clip and this is the clip to which we are becoming accustomed, we find ourselves now in a stretch where innovation and disruption are more than merely accepted, but in fact *expected*. This is a very important distinction to consider.

The *Innovator's Dilemma* — in which the incumbent is disrupted by the startup because the incumbent is correctly focused on its proven and expected offering — may itself be disrupted now. For many incumbents reinvention *is* becoming a focus and innovation has in many ways *become* the core offering — that which its customers and market now expect. Refer back to the list of transformations a few paragraphs above, and, as was previously remarked in this series, note the countless large corporations that are now launching venture initiatives and accelerator or incubation programs, (even as startups rise to incumbent status while development is still in process).

A mobile introduction is no longer a shock, artificial intelligence breakthroughs are still exciting but no longer really that surprising, a new business area may not be seen as bold as much as defensive in many cases. The absence of such events, in truth, would be the disappointment: When certain industrials reposition themselves as software companies, the market barely flinches; car manufacturers are buying into ride-sharing and self-driving cars, and the reaction is, by market standards, muted; a global investment bank launches an online deposit-taking operation, and the event is registered as though a new consumer app; a deep-learning program surpasses calculation and proves itself also at intuition (!) in a complex game, and this is news for about a week before it fades into the vague remembrance. It feels as though the questions are not as much about what the innovator-disruptor is doing, as about what else...

This is the nature of the air through which we are now cruising. When an aircraft settles in at a cruising speed it may feel to passengers like it is stationary; but, thankfully, it is not.

Staying airborne

The machinery that keeps an aircraft in flight is complex, the work is hard, and the energy required is enormous. The industrial trends showcased in this article are similarly dependent on a continuous effort of an increasingly strenuous order. As technology tends to commoditization and its economy is impacted by deflationary forces, these act like a gravitational pull that must be fought with velocity and lift:

- When disruption is *expected* and innovation is a central aspect of almost any enterprise, a steady state of movement is as important to the incumbent as it is to the startup.

- In a technology-based business — which, as suggested, is (or will be) almost all business henceforth — the core must at a minimum be perpetually refreshed, and quite likely reinvented.

- Inventiveness and its qualities — curiosity, openness, creativity, risk-taking — and the optionality that may with a bit of luck be achieved, are thus a matter of *survival*, rather than excess.

The value of an enterprise, therefore, would more than ever capture the likelihood of its subject, over time and many changes, to survive.

As all businesses, even the most mature, demonstrate aspects of new ventures today, there are venture-like *expectations* to be observed and parallels to be drawn with venture investment considerations, in all areas of the economy. Besides those contemplated in the preceding, another is the cautious and reluctant use of debt in venture capital, and the importance of preserving flexibility: Leverage is the subject of the next section.

Tools for a new trade

D. Ramsden

6. Leverage

A recurring theme in the series has been change and the velocity with which it has occurred in industry, markets, and the economy broadly. The subject of this sixth installment is structure, organization, rigidity and the constraints that such weights might place on value in the new environment.

Tools for a new trade

Institutional obligations

In periods of predictability and growth, leverage is a way to boost return, and in periods of volatility and deflationary economics it is a burden. This generalization applies to many forms of leverage, not only of the financial variety. For instance:

Borrowing and consequent obligations have their counterparts in operating leverage, a fixed cost-base to limit variable expenses that is beneficial as long as revenue grows and supports it; or in technical debt, which is a scalability in software design as long as the mechanics do not become outdated and a burden. And there are other elements in our systems that we might consider leverage, with similar or at least analogous qualities, even if we don't think of these as debt ordinarily: For instance, in academia there are departments and tenure, in government agencies there is bureaucracy, in enterprise there is the "org chart" and the meetings and reports that have to be filled out.

These fabrications are intended to support with props and structure and to enhance efficiency in what might in the other extreme be severe underperformance, or, worse, an unruly free-for-all. But it is as always a question of degree and circumstance, and while rigidity is necessary for levers to take hold, with it comes a cost that can be difficult to justify, or in some cases even ascertain, when efficiency might be better advanced with freedom. In periods of quick and constant change, it may be argued, flexibility rather than levers, is the better option.

D. Ramsden

Economy of scale

Many of the structural levers highlighted in the preceding are manifest in capital markets, which have taken on the profile and organization of increasingly sizable and structured constituencies. Partly in reflection of capital growth, partly a result of capital concentration, institutions and the markets that they form have added to an atmosphere in which *scale* is a dominant trait, at the expense of flexibility. In other words, the needed structure to support bigger and more complex markets over decades has culminated in a present state of constrained access. Here are two manifestations of this burden:

- When many growing and even profitable companies are deemed unfit (because of size) for public markets, and when many potential investors will therefore not participate in their growth, a major source of finance is out of reach for businesses, and valuable investments are out of reach for sources of liquidity. This is (very likely) an economic drain.

- The growing size of funding vehicles, driven by a system that prefers it, can also create a disadvantage, similarly marked by capital constraints, especially when financing classes are grouped into a narrow set of categories. Currently this seems to be (more or less): (a) "unicorn" seeking, (b) large profit seeking, (c) traditional asset factoring, (d) short-term speculation, (e) macro speculation, and (f) activism, with many of the participants becoming bigger and, thus, increasing their return and exposure requirement.

Tools for a new trade

The connection between these market qualities and the preceding commentary on institutional fixtures is quite direct, because a primary driver of the realities described is a structured legacy that has come to dominate market flows, and that in many ways needs to do so. This, in any case, is the simplified conclusion to an overview that has been about the funding or liability-side of the balance sheet. There is another, the business operation or the asset-side, which is summarized below.

Economics of speed

One of the effects of an economy centered around digital technology is a new freedom of movement that has spread. This can lead to volatility, in some cases, but also to new possibilities that rise to the surface quickly and take over just as fast, all enabled by an openness of information and the rapidly evolving methodology that supports it. The phenomenon is antithetical to the rigid masses previously illustrated, and, as commented at length in the prior installment in this series, it must remain so.

As we find ourselves in a period marked by *speed* and changes closely monitored by structured pools of capital, the institutional organization is often pushed to be more responsive while the entrepreneurial drive is often pulled to slow down. The resulting equilibrium is not always optimal, but the objective, always, is to find it quickly. As markets are not mere passive facilitators of price discovery and capital flows, but reflexively also impact business plans, strategic directions, executive decisions, recruitment, education, geographic and demographic trends, and other key drivers of economic value, the push and pull of capital seeking scale and velocity seeking capital may be a new defining force in markets, which comes with consequences and behaviors still in need of better understanding. It is not clear that our conventions cover the same ground.

Balancing the interests

In traditional corporate finance, the concept of match-funding indicates a link between assets and liabilities for a given enterprise. The concept determines appropriate levels of leverage, and the term and amortization rate of debt, to match the size and average life of the corresponding assets.

In an environment driven simultaneously by frantic pace, a quest for scale, deflationary economics, and structure, the matching concept may be much more delicate than it once was, as both the liability and the asset assume a profile that is different from what we have previously known. The latter now includes unknown future possibilities (as was discussed in these installments before) and the former tends now also to comprises constraints and obligations not always of financial nature (as discussed herein). If the theory still applies, it is with different parameters.

Leverage, in its assortment of structures and manifestations, is not always voluntary or controllable, but, to the extent that it is — "Deleverage," some would say, "and set the possibilities free."

Tools for a new trade

Next, a case study will be presented to illustrate the ways of navigation by one that has made it through these waters with relative success.

D. Ramsden

Tools for a new trade

D. Ramsden

7.Cycles

They say that history repeats, and those who don't know are bound to... But that is not necessarily bad, and, anyway, they don't tell us which history or in what circumstance. The past being at least as complex as the present — more so, in fact, because there is much more of it — the adage is not helpful at all. I suppose you need to learn a lot to make sense of a little, and hope that you get lucky.

It is indicated, when studying the trends and patterns of a given segment, to look at what its leadership is up to. One interpretation of one such subject with a complex history and varied possibilities is presented here.

Tools for a new trade

Product reinvestment

Around the time of Apple's acquisition of Beats, here were some principal considerations regarding the acquirer:

1. With more than $150 billion in "cash" (at the time of acquisition) and $15 billion in quarterly additions to the bank account, Apple had not made use of the excess to any meaningful extent.

2. Apple's core product, on the surface, is consumer hardware, which has become a less differentiated and more price-competitive situation to be in.

3. In short, the company competes in a commoditizing field, selling a commoditizing product, that should, in reasonable likelihood, trend cheaper with time; its defense is to add or improve features, functionality, and consumer experience... and to guard its considerable cash hoard dearly.

With that as background, the following could have been Apple's executive summary:

Proposal: Cash acquisition of a premium headphone brand that is also a streaming music service, owned and promoted by a team of notable entertainment industry figures.

Rationale:

1. Expend a seemingly large but in actuality tiny portion ($3 billion) of cash on hand...

2. to acquire a hardware accessory that is complementary to Apple's core product...

3. at a reasonable multiple of revenues (reportedly $1+ billion per year)...

4. growing the appeal (and perhaps value) of the combined consumer hardware package...

5. and in the process bring into the fold a streaming music option that may or may not be exercised (it was)...

6. while signing up a roster of entertainment notables with clout and insider connections.

Items #1–3 are financial, straight-forward, and basically sound. Items #4–5 are options (possibilities), and can't hurt. Item #6 adds to the network. Agree or disagree, as is our shared prerogative, there are some general statements in Apple's position important to consider:

- **About deflation:** Conservation of cash (and its careful and conservative use) is indicative of a deflationary mindset. With its mounting cash pile and very cautious nurturing, Apple — a leader — appears to be mindful. Thus, others should be, too. Many are.

- **About the brand:** When the distribution of content becomes commoditized — as commoditized hardware sends and receives bits through commoditized pipes and airwaves — the premium value and differentiator after features run their course, increasingly relates to image. Apple seems ready to pay for that, (and Hollywood thrown in).

- **About options:** The *possibility* of introducing new product lines or service offerings, especially if these could be integrated in a way to enhance network value, will be important to the digital enterprise. In a volatile technology environment in which consumer preferences are prone to change, the market leader is not taking its position for granted.

As of the time of this article, Apple has invested $1 billion (of its now $230 billion liquidity) in Didi Chuxing, the leading ride sharing brand in China...

Market reinvention

When Apple dropped hints about an interest in the car business, the immediate inclination by analysts and other followers was to scrutinize the rumor on the basis of the automotive sector as we know it. It was not generally appreciated, as far as I could tell, that the sector, with Apple's participation, may change.

In its history, Apple hasn't so much innovated as redesigned (maybe the distinction is arbitrary), and when this happened, the outcome was transformative beyond the product narrowly defined. The iPhone was not the first smart device at the time of its introduction, and its *pre* and *post* associations — the iPod before and iPad after — were not the first MP3 player and tablet respectively. Remarkably, Apple's involvement in the field changed everything in it.

Maybe it was the integration and continuity and elegant handoff of experiences, maybe it was the beautiful presentation, maybe it was iTunes and the App Store, maybe it was the personal touch of the retail outlets, probably all of these things, and the aura of Steve Jobs must have had its own reflexive quality. Regardless, that Apple's involvement in mobile media reshaped the field itself is now a foregone conclusion, but much more importantly, it reshaped the bigger world around it. Here is a list:

> Publishing, advertising, and entertainment; telecommunications services; retail logistics; retail style; financial services (including payments and processing); aspects of financial markets (in the immediacy and mobility of research and trading); the collection and distribution of news; education methods and possibilities; worker and workplace productivity; healthcare products and services; and, from the other side of all these things, consumer behavior, consumption patterns, and new consumer needs.

In short, anything in which mobility, immediacy, flexibility, interactivity, play a part, was (and continues to be) refashioned. There are not many categories that do not belong there in some way, and even if the device is an Android or Windows phone at this point, the idea remains: the catalyst was Apple.

Getting back to the car... It is ironic to have to say that the auto*mobile* also contains mobile qualities, but our focus has been shifted to devices (as suggested) and cars now seem a different category altogether. To be fair, the car is mobile in its own defining way — an enclosed physical space with room to spare, that moves — and thus, innovations in this field come with physical consequence, in areas of tourism, commutation, and planning; and from there, in real estate, construction, infrastructure... These are not predictions but the raising of possibilities that seem increasingly material, and it is not even essential that the subject should be Apple. There are many companies now pursuing innovation in the automotive industry.

More important are some of the lessons from Apple's past — about reflexive causes and effects, positioning, timing, and the idea that eventual winners in technology are not necessarily the innovators, but maybe the packagers, the presenters, and the skillful choreographers. A case study of one, but an important one in the digital domain, suggests: Image and possibility are sometimes interlinked, and perception may form value well beyond the first option exercise.

Grand repackaging

The term "cord cutting" is a misnomer. Referring to cable-delivered entertainment subscriptions that are cut in favor of streaming and other app-enabled services, the term implies a breaking of lines. This is a false description of what in fact takes place. The product has to be delivered somehow, so a cord (even wireless) will be necessary. Often it is still the original carrier itself.

But the issue is more profound today, because connectivity and access are part of a continuum that also includes computing, one point along which line is the device that we use to consume. This is no longer separate from that which we use to connect (like a separate set-top box and TV set, in contrast). For most of us, the combined object has tended to be our mobile computing gadget.

Truth be told, "mobility" is also a misnomer. Relating to hardware that is handheld, the word implies motion when, more correctly, it is about the possibility of motion. In fact, "mobile" devices are often (if not even mostly) used in the same stationary places as their stationary-computing counterparts. So when we refer to mobile access, what we are actually referring to is access through a device that is unplugged, and, more notably, one where the interface is increasingly a native app rather than a web browser. According to research, the ratio of the former to the latter on devices is in the 9:1 range, not even a contest.

Now, were we to reset the semantics to something that more closely resembles modernity, we may think of "cords" as services on which we would depend; and, to minimize subjectivity and questions of degree, we may sum up these utilities through the defining filter of *subscriptions*: the purchases we automatically renew. Similarly, we could redefine "mobility" to mean *app-enabled* communication, for reasons cited. Taken in combination, thus, *subscription-based and app-enabled* services are highly significant for purposes of this discussion... about cords and our mobility and Apple:

Among Apple's recent product and strategic announcements, some of the most notable have been (a) greater diversity of glass size (i.e., bigger or smaller tablets, bigger or smaller phones), and (b) new rental plans to finance purchases or to stream. There is, in other words, an expansion of accessibility and app-enabled consumption categories to suit all tastes and styles, even in the enterprise, and there is the offering of everything as a subscription service.

Tools for a new trade

As redefined, this is a new "cord" that, in combination with the App Store, replicates many of the old "cord" functions — a cable set-top box and channels — shepherding these into an era of Apple's formulation. The new network might, one day, promote other selections from its lineup — the laptop, watch, headphones, TV, maybe at some point, the car — as a package of ubiquity, so to speak, as a subscription service. (The cash is in place to fund the consumer offer on credit terms, and not a bad use during deflation.)

When that day comes, we might look back on "cord cutting" as so much quaint naiveté, because the truer cord will just then have been tied.

This article was about Apple, to some extent, but also about others and their respective legacies: the search engine, the carrier, the messenger, the publisher, the retailer, the finance company, and everyone...

Next up: a look at all from the perspective of markets that judge.

D. Ramsden

Tools for a new trade

D. Ramsden

8. Markets

The market rises and the market sets, and hurries back to where it rises. It blows to the south and turns to the north; round and round, ever returning on its course. What has been will be again, and there is nothing new under the sun...

But there is such a plentitude of permutations.

An inherent topic in this series about digital economics has been the vastness of those numbers, while the subject of this eighth chapter is the market ebb and flow and certain signals in the fluctuation.

Tools for a new trade

In transition

The year 2016 began with a global market pattern that many referred to as "turmoil," which eased into a rebound later on and which for the past several months has spiked and troughed in waves within what seems to be a trading range of sorts. That anyway is what the index chart would show, (but there are doubters). The net change to date: not much.

Oil prices, economy stagnation, China, politics, and, as seems now to be a fixture since the dawn of time, action or the absence of it by central banks on all sides of every ocean, these things have tended to dominate the headlines from one day to the next. The messages and their dissection, the *algo*s digesting text and fund managers talking their book, are churning fast and wide on our networks and devices, adding to the excitement of a market that is, as mentioned, back where it started. But that is a superficial read, and anyway the causality is unclear, possibly even circular.

Under the surface of this persistent multitude of factors that may be fundamental on some level, there are traces of a different volatility acting on the system, which is not noticeable in the charts. When Icahn and Tepper and Tiger Global, for instance, are sellers of what Berkshire Hathaway is buying; when Soros is long gold because of *deflationary* concerns; when fund managers voice pessimism that reaches alarmist levels although price multiples continue to be historically record-setting; and when ventures are marked up or down by double-digit percentages, and then back again, without catalyst; that may all signify a thing that is not turmoil, strictly speaking, as much as inconstancy. The distinction may seem vague but is in my opinion important: If turmoil is akin to choppy waters, inconstancy may be a bit like floating over steady seas without a rudder.

One interpretation is this: The market described is a market in transition — from old to new economies extending their reach — for which central monetary props have been a sort of camouflage. It is, I think, significant that monetary intervention on one hand, and widespread industrial and consumption changes on the other, have generally coincided. (That "software is eating the world" was famously reported by Marc Andreessen in 2011, a few months after the Fed launched QE2.) In their respective ways these have been the defining milestones of our time, for both the market and economy that it (in theory) reflects.

The undertow

It was tempting and maybe necessary over the period referenced, to have watched the flow of capital — both private and public — and stared googly-eyed at headline grabbing funding rounds and "unicorns" and the social media IPOs and the explosion of startups that was not like the dot-com bubble this time, because now the selection process was more discerning and the traction generally real. In the finer print, however, there was a more challenging dynamic settling into financial markets, particular to analytic estimation and value recognition, which in the end has consequence in strategy and competition in all the underlying sectors. The difficulty is one of capturing key metrics in financial models (that in principle drive capital flows), and the challenge pertains to differences from custom: the business formula and methodology are not what they used to be, and the science is still being tested.

Below is an illustrative list of the new puzzle pieces, many of which have been touched upon in prior entries here:

- Digital technology is built on operations and directions that are often still in process of trial and error.

- Category convergences are leading to uncertainties of comparison and competitive peer group assessment.

- Ongoing business transformations are (more than typically) stifling the credibility of financial forecasts.

- Blurring lines between incumbents and disrupters are leading to the same in the discounting of risk.

- Innovation is driving down costs and also revenue potential in a deflationary pattern that is uneven.

- "Winner-take-most" fundamentals are increasing the precondition of scale, which can be hard to predict, and sustain.

As is always the case in finance — and this new era is no exception — the overarching rule is supply and demand. But in the digital economy in question, which is predicated on a unit (the digital bit) that can be produced and reproduced without limit and distributed virtually anywhere instantly, that basic economic equilibrium is altered.

By way of contrast, consider the quantities to which our analytics had become accustomed for a long time prior: the stone, the grain, the yard, the barrel, the metric ton, the railway car, the bullion, the channel lineup, the city size, the market rank... In short, the list of changes and transitions points to something far more fundamental to financial markets than, say, a change in growth rate, profit margins, or valuation range. The event, in fact, is one of a general recalibration — of a system that is very big and at the same time sort of dizzy.

Emerging focal points

But markets are by definition adaptable, even if certain circumstances take longer than others to internalize. So it is possible already to discern the semblance of a method that is taking shape as swings and turns from one day to the next, or quarter to quarter, might seem disorienting. Three areas in particular stand out, having started to come into focus, and to outline a shape in our field of vision to which market attention is increasingly drawn. This is not always purposeful, not always consistent, but seems more and more universal and with an attitude that approaches understanding:

- **Networks**: In this new economy driven by the connectivity of systems, the nature of networks — their nodes and clusters, their combinations and splits, the robustness or malleability of different types, and their very definitions — requires a great deal of attention. We are accustomed to thinking of networks strictly in the sense of communication, but as connectivity becomes the dominant quality in all sectors, so also the concept of a network is being revisited. Its value is a key driver in the enterprise and elsewhere, and not all networks are equivalent in effect, we begin to realize.

- **Options**: Defining this to signify undeveloped, likely unknown, perhaps unknowable possibilities that exist in an enterprise and elsewhere, and considering the concept in the strategic rather than the trading sense of calls and puts, there is a very real correspondence to value (creation as well as destruction) associated with optionality. In a time of massive transformation, these unknowns take on special significance. The Black-Scholes formula is not what is required to make sense of strategic valuation, but its basis in volatility as a positive attribute deserves to be acknowledged in a volatile time.

- **Currency**: What constitutes a store of value and medium of exchange has been scrutinized quite extensively with the emergence of cryptocurrency, but more fundamentally still (and contained in the idea of the blockchain) is the notion of information itself as a currency. In an age of mechanized knowledge that is at once accessible and highly liquid, conceptions about value and exchange are being revisited. The formation or erosion of capital is increasingly and more immediately linked to data — which, like the blockchain itself, has become a distributed resource.

The three areas summarized are interconnected and not listed in order of importance necessarily. Rather, these make up a whole that could be a cause, effect, or both, in a system based on digital traffic flows, reflected in the foggy mirror of financial markets, based on the same.

In subsequent segments these subjects will be expanded upon with examples and further questions that arise.

Tools for a new trade

D. Ramsden

9.Resources

In the previous section, on markets, a state of what may be disorientation was described. New influences were noted in a newly digitized economy that has only just begun to be observed at scale. Two of these new areas requiring focused consideration were identified broadly as networks and options. In this current article the two are explored further, concluding that the market disorientation may not be entirely unjustified.

The elements

Before proceeding to the topical discussion, an introduction to the characters: A *network*, for our purposes, is a system of objects (nodes) interconnected through a web of common links; such properties as clustering, directions, and degrees are not dealt with in this article, but we accept that these are critical in determining the nature of the network. We also note that *network effect* is a quality by which a network becomes more valuable for the whole as individual utilization increases. An *option* is a possibility that may or may not materialize, or, as is conventional to say in finance, may or may not be exercised. These broad and rudimentary definitions are intended to aid in a general overview; and, in keeping with such generalities, the discussion becomes most interesting if we should consider the broadest interpretations of what is a network and what is an option, beyond the conventions of telecom and financial markets.

We can imagine a scenario in which every business is a software business. The pace of industrial innovation is fast, the reach of distribution is broad, the level of competition is deep, and the possibility of disruption is material. In this scenario, there are aspects of the startup in even the most mature enterprise. That is also to say that all finance has aspects of venture capital then, to a greater or lesser extent, and all financiers would have something to learn from venture capitalists. The idea was broached in these articles before, because we are getting to that point, if not already there.

There is a value system in the environment described, in which networks and options are centrally important to venture capitalists. This could be summarized as follows: For value preservation and the formation of a stable base (realizing that stability is relative in such a fast-paced software marketplace), there is the network. It is characterized by resilience because its mesh can be difficult to render obsolete, unlike the individual pieces of technology that supports it. For outsized return potential, which is critical to venture capital considering the risk of technology non-adoption and obsolescence, there is optionality. This often (but not always) is born from new inventions. Both of these areas might assume different forms, depending on the nature of the enterprise, and both of these have their evolving connotations in a fluid climate, such as the one depicted.

The manifestations

To illustrate, a few examples from the actual: Facebook relies on its social network(s) to build out options in areas like virtual reality, video distribution, and messaging. Google, benefiting from a different sort of network effect in search and information cataloguing, is investing in automotive and medical innovation and other new fields from the springboard of its networked data and data science know-how that it has developed. Amazon, the network of which may be closer in nature to Google than Facebook, takes pride in launching high-risk high-return new lines of business, or even trying to do so at a loss. When the attempt pays off and the option is exercised, we have such new enormities as Amazon Web Services.

These samples were arbitrarily selected, in no order of preference. Not all technology companies benefit from network effect, just as not all networks are building optionality. Many of the more valuable enterprises, however, when dissected in this fashion, tend to reveal a composition that is similar to the illustration. And increasingly, companies that were not considered technology businesses, certainly not software, are moving in the direction (e.g., GE, Goldman Sachs, Ford), and thus the formula is likely to apply — in varying ways and degrees — in an expanding circle.

What seems more mysterious for now — although one would expect advances with time and research — is a method for calculating the economics; a way to financially evaluate networks and business optionality that is more than intuitive. While traditional options pricing may provide us with a start at strategic optionality, but really very little more than that in the context of illiquid assets and limited diversification, so also we derive initial benefit from academic studies in areas of networks and their effects (e.g., as popularized by Duncan Watts). Such studies incorporate their own mesh of interrelated fields — in sociology, information systems, and economics — and we have therefore begun, we think, to understand the basics of what makes the organism live. The relationship, however, between biology and formulaic valuation, so to speak, is a financial exercise that would at best be still primitive.

The gaps

Below is a set of questions about networks to underscore unknowns that come to mind, which could be worth a closer look in theory and practice:

1. Are there financial metrics that can be expressed in relation to network structure, and can these be standardized and tested universally?

2. Are there quantifiable relationships between a network's elements and economic output or potential?

3. How do such quantities and ratios change as networks do over time?

4. How do the costs of network formation and growth vary with its form and features?

5. Might network effect also break a network? And can this possibility be estimated as a cost to hedge or to offset?

6. Can there be networks that do not follow such rules and principles, if these were formulated, and should such entities really be deemed networks?

These questions do not lend themselves to easy research, but the proliferation of networks in our modern economy — of the social, commercial, technical, financial, and industrial varieties — is increasing the sample size of analysis, as well as our perspective. It may also become apparent, in time, that certain manifestations that had not been recognized as networks actually are, while some networks actually aren't — both of which values presently miscalculated, perhaps.

Optionality is in some ways more pedestrian, depending on perspective, and its relation to strategy and business investment is an area that more closely resembles traditional corporate finance. For a given project, the analysis would include: long-term return potential; risk mitigation and expense control; strategic cross-development opportunity; portfolio diversification; capital cost assessment; and, perhaps most importantly, market communication and acceptance. (We note the corporate examples cited earlier, and, in a phenomenon that is in ways related, the proliferation of venture capital bloggers that has emerged in the past decade.)

Although implementation may appear straight-forward, as these things go, the outcomes are necessarily uncertain. It takes a special kind, and some companies seem to have raced ahead of others — because of their origins in disruption? — in their acceptance that the core business could be entirely reinvented in this fashion. And probably needs to be.

By the same token, certain investors seem more conscious, more in tune than others with the new realities, and the volatile unpredictability that forms a special value mathematics: sustained by a terrain of network elements and the oxygen of options.

Next: a further consideration of examples, to dig into an area closely related to all the above — the life expectancy of the enterprise.

D. Ramsden

Tools for a new trade

D. Ramsden

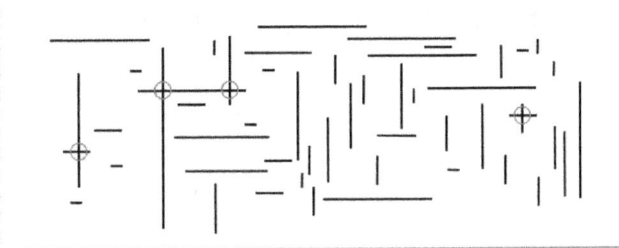

10.Term

In previous sections of this series, inefficiencies were discussed in relation to definitions and comparisons, when a transition is underway in virtually all known categories.

An illustration of the challenge is a market clustering, observed around the beginning of 2016, of so-called FANG stocks — Facebook, Amazon, Netflix and Google — which at least temporarily seemed to act as points of reference for each other. Differences in business model aside, which are numerous, there is another (related) difference, having to do with life expectancy.

In the current article we consider this idea through the lens of network character and its optionality (as introduced in the prior episode) with a special look at two FANGs.

Tools for a new trade

Facebook and the asset's future

The case used to be straight-forward. At one polar end there is the technology, which requires continuous defense, reinvention and upgrade in order to survive. Technology companies depend on innovation. At the other extreme there is the network, which is robust because it has effect and there are switching costs for its users, who preserve the value of its base with their interconnected presence. At one end there is high volatility (and enhanced option value), at the other there are elements of stability and leverage.

The argument is no longer so concise. When the world's largest social network makes it a point to acquire several up-comers, at increasing prices, at first for a mere 1% of its market capitalization but later for 10% — in the examples of Instagram and WhatsApp respectively — this is a signal from inside that the network cannot be taken for granted. Maybe it means that the effect is not what it once was, or that the network needs to be expanded and multiplied in order to last. Perhaps, as well, it may have been suggested that software networks are subservient to hardware, so that home-screen real estate on the controlling devices is valuable property to purchase.

Regardless of the rationale, (it might be any and all of the above, or others), when the dominant social network buys a small one, the transaction is a symbol. When the price is high, the message is not subtle. When the payment is in stock, there is a statement in that as well, because a buyer with multiple and ample resources will use the least expensive to transact, (echoing the economic notion that cash is particularly dear during commoditized deflationary phases). And when the successful up-comer quickly sells to the deeper pocket with the greater resources, there is in that as well a sort of message, possibly about necessity.

While the idea of category convergences has been a recurring theme in this series of essays, the reference was usually to industry segments. In the present scenario, however, another convergence is showcased: the thematic blend of network and technology, whereby the former assumes the volatile insecurities of the latter. The notion is introduced that networks in the digital age may have a life expectancy of diminishing duration.

Facebook's subsequent acquisition of Oculus and its bet on virtual reality as a next social networking phase is consistent with the thesis… at least in a survey size of one. In fairness, however, this one has proven itself to know digital networks better than most, for now.

Netflix and the nature of the base

Is it an entertainment production company? A premium cable service? A distribution outlet? A hub? An over-the-top video product? A retailer? Is it largely or a little bit of all these things? Maybe, but not to the same extent, and narrowly each one comes with its special risks, competitors, and value drivers; all of which are currently in flux. If only Netflix were a network, it could be grounded thus and safer in its "moat," fending off competitors most effectively. Some think that Netflix is just that.

At one time it was commonplace to refer to the video content distributor as a network. In the sense of unified outlets and brand presence this may have been correct. But in the modern-day connotation of network graphs and directional clusters, the terminology is less straight-forward.

It is not merely a question of semantics, but one of economic preservation and defensibility. Nor is it a binary yes or no question, but one of nuance and qualitative details that determine the value of this base — its asset and the options that emerge from it. What kind of network is Netflix?

If it is indeed a network, it is predominantly unidirectional, like a broadcaster, which is less sticky than the bidirectional variety because the worth of the asset is not increased by interaction. And the switching costs for a subscriber are less constraining. In an environment of freely flowing digital bits, distribution mechanisms are not especially defensible when a better or more popular alternative surfaces.

In this line of scrutiny, Netflix is not alone, in fact it is almost marginal in the greater context. Apple, Amazon, Microsoft, IBM, even Twitter, which calls itself a social network, are at similar defining junctures. So also the banking and finance sector, healthcare, education, manufacturing, transportation. All of these segments that are transitioning to software business models, if not already there, will very likely be faced with the same necessary assessment: Is it a network, if so, what kind and what would its economic substance be? And if not, how likely is it to continue in its present form within the commoditization that is spreading all around it?

A question of survival

The introductory passage of this article made reference to imperfect comparisons between certain businesses. What followed were two case specific illustrations (that may seem disjointed), profiling two companies that for some appear to belong to the same digital media category. The point of it was not as much to underscore differences in business model and strategy, as important to comparison as such things are, but to bring to the forefront an aspect that underlies the valuation of any growing enterprise: the implied notion of *perpetuity*.

It is a large word, so large that it often goes unnoticed, even as the present value of a business asset is dominated by its expected economic productivity *forever*. Perpetuity is always assumed, for in the other alternative the asset would be depleting by nature, or in some other way expected to cease. This is almost never predicted, even though history is replete with enterprises that have ended. Or, if they still exist, they do so in a wholly different form from what had been their origin.

In a digital economy, the risk (although not new) is much more real than ever, because the pace of change has quickened and the term to a finality (whether as an end or as a transformation) has been abbreviated. Notions about networks and technology, assets and optionality, reinvention and survival, are now as immediate to the valuation exercise as cash flows and the near-term forecast model itself.

In the next section, such and similar ideas as thus far covered in the series with respect to individual business forms, will be expanded out into the economic aggregate, reflecting on general consequences in the macro atmosphere.

Tools for a new trade

D. Ramsden

11. Diffusion

Out of prior commentary about business strategy and valuation in a digital technology environment, in the current installment more general global issues are tackled, or circled for approach in any case.

Measuring a new economy by old economy standards is problematic, I believe, and the management and architecture of new macro growth on the basis of old macro science — which is in any case more truly an art, as everyone knows — will yield prescriptions that might only work by accident. This is not to suggest that a new economics will necessarily open a new path, because economics never necessarily does anything; but maybe the probability will rise in our favor.

In contrast with previous chapters in this series, which tend to a more methodical style, the present segment is a sort of mosaic, and in its way perhaps more daring. It is a call to action, among other things, from the cheap seats where the diehard fans are always gathered.

Consequence of lightness

In chemistry *diffusion* signifies the movement of atoms or molecules from an area of higher concentration to an area of lower concentration. An economy based on the gathering and processing of information and the wide dissemination of resulting bits, is an economy of diffusion: Its markets are diffuse markets.

In physics *diffusion* refers to the process by which molecules intermingle as a result of their energy of random motion. An economy bound and intertwined through dense global networks in which mechanized information is stored or flows and sometimes explodes, is an economy of diffusion: Its commerce is a diffuse commerce.

When analysts consider supply and demand in such a new economy, depicted qualities must be taken in consideration. Diffusion creates a special economic context, where one can no longer always wrap one's arms around an economic good, and squeeze. This is a big deal and causes a big difference in the math we used to learn.

A limitless coexistence

In this context — which is a context of software that "is eating the world," as monumentally reported in 2011 — there are few constraints on motion; and identical particles can exist in multiple locations simultaneously. When everything is everywhere, as it were, abundance is not meaningful, or at least not in the traditional sense. Scarcity, by the same token, is maybe a matter of *depth*, but not necessarily quantity. Scarcity and abundance, measured in levels of supply and demand, is the basis of all economics.

―――

The principles of prior eras will seem different, sometimes even strange, in this evolving world. Supply and demand, as noted, and the very idea of markets and commerce, are being refashioned. The formulas may not be obsolete, but should at the very least be revisited, and maybe then retargeted or refocused. Inflation may now prove artificial, and deflation the natural tendency; productivity, employment, exports and imports, may be altogether rediscovered as new and different.

―――

Business readapts to diffuse systems: Imagine a scenario in which no one along the supply chain, not the merchant, the distributor, the producer, not anyone, is concerned with "shelf space." Because there are no shelves; there is only digital attention.

―――

In this world the distinction between vendor and consumer fades, and on some level everyone is an owner-investor: Often, however, only in oneself, which is a portfolio with new and different characteristics.

―――

Tools for a new trade

The noted effects are not limited to economics in the material sense. There are psychological, social and cultural adaptations and consequences, of greater or lesser velocity, which intertwine reflexively with economics and its branches. We all feel it in our daily lives, in our habits and our work, in our interactions.

―――

While all this is a matter of proportion, with certain aspects more actual than others, it is also a depiction of where we will universally find ourselves if current trends persist. All said and done, that is the very subject (and reason for being) of economics.

Constraints upon the bit

In one practical sense, the preceding comments relate to central planning — of monetary and fiscal policy — which impacts every market directly (as we have in the past decade had an opportunity to observe). The debate, however, is lagging, or is at most peripheral to such issues. While their complexity would not lead to any quick resolution, or at all to some quick study, it is concerning that the process has not in earnest begun — not in the mainstream — even with evidence of massive changes mounting all around us. Marketplaces, transfers, augmented reality, artificial intelligence, robots, autonomous transport, quantum computing, are byproducts of the same essential flow, which is not showing any sign of diminution. This begs for a whole new multi-disciplinary investigation.

As the new economy described is an event that has sprung almost out of nowhere and taken over in almost no time, it's understandable that it could be awhile before our big and well-developed systems adapt, even if our individual little ones do so in our little malleable ways much faster. In an earlier installment, on leverage, there was discussion about rigid systems that benefit from structure in times of stability: The present time, however, is not that, and resistance is disadvantageous.

In yet other articles of this series, repeated reference was made to networks and options, to convergences between traditional industry segments, to convergences between financial asset classes, and to new organizations that operate to build value against the two-fold challenge of limitless supply and deflationary commoditized technology. Classical economics, regardless of school, is not always accommodating to such notions, and the glimmers of inspiration that one comes across are at best suggestive, rarely even economic. Maybe for that very reason, comparatively profound:

- *The fragment on machines*, Karl Marx — an early look into knowledge and free time as forms of capital;

- *The work of art in the age of mechanical reproduction*, Walter Benjamin — commentary on image commoditization and supply;

- *Post-Capitalist Society*, Peter Drucker — knowledge work and its dominance of modern industry (not yet having observed mass mechanization of knowledge at the time of publication);

- *Agapē Agape*, William Gaddis — reflections on formula, nuance, the collective, and the individual;

- *Zero to One*, Peter Thiel — the venture capital perspective as a new strategic vision;
- *The Hard Thing About Hard Things*, Ben Horowitz — the executive in an unstable atmosphere;
- *Collective dynamics of 'small-world' networks*, Duncan Watts & Steven Strogatz — as some networks have grown large, the world is becoming smaller, as if by algorithm;
- *Cities and The Wealth of Nations*, Jane Jacobs — the thesis could be reinterpreted, with cities and networks analogously interchangeable;
- *Crowds and Power*, Elias Canetti — multitudes and diffusion being as closely paired as they are.

The material is searchable, and everywhere, as has already been mentioned.

The next section will continue with a phenomenon that counterbalances and is in part made possible by diffusion: *Concentration* and data treasures that accumulate.

D. Ramsden

Tools for a new trade

D. Ramsden

12. Concentration

This is a companion piece to the previous entry in the series, in which the idea of diffusion was introduced as an important new element in the digitized economy.

In this current episode, we take a closer look at data that is born and passed around in the diffusion: its qualities and flows and new formations, which are, in ways, akin to banks.

Tools for a new trade

Data qualities and quantities

In an information economy built on digital technology, data can be a store of value and, sometimes, a medium of exchange. Its collection is a form of capital, which can be traded, sold, invested, and is subject to value swings like other such forms, although more liquid and transferable given its digital nature. Unlike money, however, which shares some similar traits, the data asset is not fungible. This makes it more valuable to some, and less valuable to many. (Fungibility—the property of individual units that are capable of mutual substitution—is a distinctive feature of money. For data, on the other hand, such fungibility would be a flaw.)

The value store that is data in a digital information economy is rather like an entity that evolves, expands, sometimes changes its appearance or loses our attention. And it assumes a different role, becomes a different character, based on context and the company it keeps. I am not a data scientist, but this is what I have observed:

- Individual data *points* have their individual and unique qualities
- Individual data *sets* have certain individual and *dynamic* qualities
- *Combinations* of data sets create *new dimensions* with new qualities
- New *dimensions* can enhance the value of individual data points
- The cycle repeats in a loop this way, or can launch new directions

The progression is almost geometric, from point to line to plane to sphere as dimensions multiply and the levels deepen. But where geometry is a clean, almost sterile ideal, the described data cycle and the life forms that emerge from it — behavior recognition, analytics and targeting, navigation, language processing, learning, diagnosis, the various permutations and derivatives of all that — are messier and maybe more biological in nature... at least until visually represented, which can be deceptively simple at times.

Composition of new banks

The possibilities of data and the value of its signals — in practice as well as theory — are in perpetual flux as particles move through the diffusion, in many ways like money flows that enable and support economies. And as money flows lead to capital formation, so also data flows form massive concentrations (as already suggested).

Imagine a net cast in an ocean of flowing data, collecting all the little swimming bits around and giving rise to a new ecosystem of data sets in its capture. This entity may have started small and grown through aggregation, or maybe with the multiplicity and evolution of its dynamic data calculations as these grew more intricate and took on new dimensions. The described formation thus becomes an island and over time a continent with mountains and cities and big movements.

We give these movements names like machine learning and AI, and know the giant structures by their brands: such as Google and Facebook and Apple and Amazon; or IBM, Microsoft and, I don't know, Goldman Sachs; GE is maybe on its way. These own (or are) data masses and related toolkits for sorting and management, which preserve and grow their mineral density through scale economies and unique network effects. Sometimes there are also other vessels that spring up to do the same, or seek to. And sometimes the networks decay and the dilapidated structures fall, where new ones emerge out of the rubble. Every so often, as well, the structures are made of fragile matter, risking collapse with the merest stirring; say, a new technology that comes along, or a new feature in demand, a new dimension, or a breach.

Too deep to fail

As stores of value, the good ones, the deep ones, are few, and very big. These are the ones to watch, the giants that dominate the diffusion. The title of this section is an allusion to banking debates that have taken place for some time, where "too big to fail" has been a sort of warning. In the present case, although there could be some of that, the tag line is as aptly a description, a natural state of the massive data troves that strengthen by virtue of their mass.

The network effects that some analysts and business strategists obsess over, that has been a subject in this series almost every chapter it seems, is now most valuable, most potent, and most difficult to break when it is built on data dynamism. Usage begets increased usage, which begets increased collections of data and new or deeper dimensions as previously sketched out, which leads to new offerings and value for both the vendor and the customer. Which leads to usage and increased usage, and so on from the top. The statement thus — too deep to fail — is transcending allusion and taking over in reality:

More than half of the world's top-ten companies by market value are among those mentioned previously in the article. This is the new wealth — made of data stores in varying degrees, in an economy characterized by diffuse information flows and capture.

───────────────

Next, aspects of strategic investment and portfolio composition will be the subject (with examples), based on the above and all the preceding commentary in the series.

Tools for a new trade

D. Ramsden

13. Portfolio

In a period of volatility, investment and speculation are closely paired. During a time of constant change, business building and portfolio development are by necessity conjoined. The digital economy and its phenomena that run parallel, as previously outlined throughout this long essay, have set the stage thus.

The current episode elaborates on these notions and raises questions that seem appropriate to ask.

Tools for a new trade

Diversified long-term hold

The links between business strategy and investment, and between investment and speculation — by association, therefore, between strategy and speculation — have always been direct. There are always speculative considerations in strategy just as there are elements of uncertainty in investment. Such connections are always relative and a matter of proportion, and the extent to which secondary or qualifying factors in a stable time dominate a period of instability, is a question of emphasis. The emphasis, today, appears to be pronounced. Two samples follow.

In Warren Buffett's 2016 letter to Berkshire Hathaway shareholders there is the following commentary, in reference to technology trends that impact us all: "Productivity gains frequently cause upheaval: Both capital and labor can pay a terrible price when innovation or new efficiencies upend their worlds... Investors who diversify widely and simply sit tight with their holdings are certain to prosper..."

There are many (moving) pieces packed in this one blurb, but one feels as though the word "investors" was not arbitrarily selected. In Buffett's synopsis of the complex situation, speculation can be reduced through diversification, and further mitigated by patience. The idea is not new, but there is novelty in the context.

Around the same time as the posting of the Berkshire letter, an interview with Mark Zuckerberg was published, in which the founder and CEO offers the following about Facebook's perspective on new directions for the company: "There's a long-term question and a short-term question... People often say that it is easier to predict the way things are going to be 10 to 20 years in the future than to predict how it is going to be 3 years from now... We are betting that people will always want more immersive ways to express themselves... Soon it will be [virtual reality], I bet."

It was tempting to highlight the repeated use of the word "bet" in this passage, but maybe that would have been too subjective an editorial emphasis. In any case, the CEO's uncertainty is explicit in his reference to time horizon, even if speculation is only hinted at by what may be an accidental choice of words. Zuckerberg would seem to agree with Buffett in his favoring the longer term over the short, and both risk-takers appear like-minded in their probabilistic approach to looking out. There is a difference between the two, perhaps, in Facebook's ability to diversify to the extent that Berkshire Hathaway is able to do, but the social network has been working to change that with new offerings (e.g., virtual reality, as is stated).

The point is this: Where the portfolio manager ends and the business executive begins, where hold period takes over from strategic vision, and the extent to which the job is about (thoughtful) speculation, are questions that flow, perhaps rhetorically, from the cases at hand. As mentioned, the rhetoric may have been less loud in a time of lesser instability.

Concentrated short-term risk

A separate issue — more subtle but more universal — is discernible in the selected passages: That is the evolving dynamic between individual and enterprise, and the emerging profile of the consumer-employee in a new form. When the nature of the enterprise is perpetually changing, and possibly even speculative, the employee assumes a risk that is itself not far removed from speculation. The skills that are learned and the experience that can be leveraged are both exposed to changes in business direction, to economic transformations, and to industrial disruptions. Were these changes to occur over decades, as had been the rule for some time, the risk would be more purely associated with Buffett's long-term investment perspective. When changes, however, happen in years, or sometimes even faster, we start to push against Zuckerberg's short-term concerns. The Berkshire Hathaway passage on investment, portfolio diversification and long horizon, concludes, ironically, thus: "A long-employed worker [on the other hand] faces a different equation."

The implication is that the difference is not to the employee's advantage. Perhaps the purest way to illustrate the dynamic is in the interaction of technology founder-entrepreneur and the venture capital syndicate that supports him or her financially. On one side — that of the founder — an investor in a speculative portfolio of one, while on the other side, a diversified pool, with plenty of time, a great deal of updated comparative analysis, and many pearls of wisdom...

Whether in reaction or as a driver, the digital upheaval that gave rise to startups like Facebook, and social media more broadly, has also coincided with new consumer-employee possibilities. Marketplaces, the gig economy, the sharing economy — all popular designations for individual enterprise and forms of labor in which *the firm* is effectively disintermediated (or more correctly, replaced) — are manifestations of the same event: the investment of the individual in oneself and the beginnings of personal diversification to address the speculative risks involved.

Questions of perspective

As the global economy continues to transition from decades of industrial tradition to one of digitized knowledge and its networked distribution, from a relation between capital and labor that was reasonably well defined to a new digital format of which the full economic impact is not yet understood, the risk-return considerations outlined are likely to assume greater immediacy — for institutions and individuals alike. As this happens, our views and questions would naturally readapt, and answers we invent should probably be framed in a new perspective.

Here is a sampling of some that come to mind, in one way or another embedded in Buffett's and Zuckerberg's commentaries, or at least in one interpretation of these, as noted:

- How would the reclassification of investment and speculation in a time of massive change impact the definition of what is strategy, tactics, and execution?

- How would portfolio theory be incorporated into business vision, also as distinctions between stages in business life-cycle change?

- What constitutes a strategic investment if enterprise should assume the profile of a speculative portfolio?

- What is the new relationship between enterprise and labor when each increasingly becomes a portfolio holding of the other?

- Can portfolio theory and investment management be expanded from capital to labor, and if so, how does this redefine the financial asset?

The teachings of the trade

Before all that, however, we continue to study and hopefully learn some things, as there is so much that remains a mystery even in basic finance, let alone more heady fields like strategy and economics. While it may seem that speculation is akin to gambling, a matter of chance, there is a lot that we can learn from those who have been very good at it, or their students. For instance, Soros on reflexivity, Dalio on cycles, Icahn on pragmatism, Livermore on momentum, Taleb on "black swans," Lewis on history, and thus and so on through the canon.

But as this article and the series of which it is a part are principally about fundamental business building and financing rather than the secondary market trade, we close off the discussion with two passages that, I believe, echo a few of the sentiments and ideals that were shared.

1. Charlie Munger, February 2016 (the context is not important, because more or less universal): "What you have now is sort of a venture capital operation in the software business and the tag-end remnants of [a legacy business] attached. For you Ben Graham groupies, you're in new territory, [and] if it works you don't really deserve it."

2. Jeff Bezos, frequently and in different settings (although the percentages sometimes rise): "I think there's a 70% chance you're going to lose all your

money, so don't invest unless you can afford to lose it... That's a very liberating expectation, expecting to fail."

Amazon, like Berkshire Hathaway, has become an enormously valuable portfolio. There are profound lessons to be learned from both, for all of us.

_____

The next chapter will be the last in this 14-part essay on digital economics. Its subject, loosely, will be the value of transcending formula in an increasingly algorithmic environment.

Tools for a new trade

D. Ramsden

14. Specialization

This is the last episode. I hope that those who stuck it out through the series found the articles to be consistently interesting and at times even entertaining. If, in addition, these were informative once or twice, I hope the shelf-life of that element will not be short, as trends and circumstances continue to evolve.

The current installment is addressed to the entrepreneurs especially — but in the broadest and most inclusive sense. It might be interpreted between the lines as an offering of advice, but that is not at all the case: (1) Far be it from me, (2) I don't want the responsibility, (3) or the liability, or (4) the competition. Some of these disclaimers may be mutually exclusive, I'm not sure, or possibly redundant. But, as I have often heard it said, it is better to be safe than sorry. So let's chalk this one up to entertainment (i.e., my own).

Tools for a new trade

Attentiveness to flux

In this series about digital economics, a recurring theme has been the parallel phenomena of massive and widespread transformations underway and the convergence of categories that used to be more distinct than they have become. In the industrial flux (mirrored in finance and markets) one senses that, as time passes, the separations between shapes are fading and the colors are blending, resulting in a collective that is in tone and texture more like a fluid mix than a dry mosaic. This is happening on every canvas.

Fund transfer is turning into messaging, which are commerce and media respectively, in turn producing and using data to substantiate both finance and promotion to complete the commercial loop. Manufacturing is becoming robotics, which can be printed and assembled as a software exercise. These machines connect through networks that are more or less the ones connecting our devices, now worn or pocketed or used to store perishables. Mobility (including physical transport), the referenced connectivity, and energy are beginning to blend, as battery power and other renewable sources improve, which in turn leads to use cases in the home or other real estate that can easily be retrofitted for ubiquitous and flexible independence. This, and the new car model, are a software update away, while the devices on our wrists bring healthcare to the networked mix in more sophisticated ways with every version. Increasingly the difference between these access points is one of size, especially that of the glass that is touched, which alone seems to define the super-computer's scope and temperament. That is a simplification, I know, but the image is what matters in this argument.

Even if some version of the singularity to which such information-driven flows might lead is still a long way out, the depicted transformations and convergences are not. These are actual and clear, immediate, and impacting the world with regularity and completeness. Thus, while it is (still) unfair to say that specialization in a given category is outmoded, the subject has been complicated by changing fields and demarcations. (Please refer to the suggestive commentary in *note 1* below, or hold the thought and read through until you get there). Specialization is more nuanced now, to say the least, and in important ways requires a revisit. Narrow footprints may not (yet) be obsolete, but have their limitations.

The point of a terrain

It is common in the world of startup enterprise to refer to a change in course as a "pivot." The idea is similar in certain sports where the player might change direction abruptly, such as in basketball where one stationary leg stands at the center of angular rotations by the other. In these activities, however, and certainly in basketball, the ground is firm, and it is this robustness that enables the pivot to happen.

Now, when terrain is varied, versatile, more than a geometric plane but sometimes unpredictable in depth and angle, it is less correct to still refer to one's abrupt redirection as a pivot. A rebalancing, perhaps... and, when seeing the result from this perspective, the pivot is more a reflex than a premeditated act, a necessary reorientation that, in the best and ideal case, might be anticipated and prepared for as though a frame of mind. Such preparation is

The future as a filter

"One must be absolutely modern," according to the poet and entrepreneur (*note 3*).

It was easier to become modern in those days, when modernity turned over no more than once a generation. One had time to settle in and polish one's pose, and to be expert in the particular novelty. When conditions perpetually change, however, the most up-to-date trendsetter is at risk of turning passé at almost any moment. (I am sure that I have seen this happen.)

It is hard work to stay modern in our circumstance. It is not something you do once and then forget about, like getting a degree or moving downtown. It is something to refresh, it is continuous and an ongoing education. One must not only understand one's present time, but one must gather particles of the future. It is really like investing, which is doubly difficult today because it is not just some asset whose prospects one needs to estimate, but that very same asset in an ever changing context.

Some things that may be still considered modern in the world will not be so for much longer. The specialization of greatest value then is not technology or commerce or a given field that supports these, but in the blend of all that, just in case; not the art or science, but both, to understand; not the history or the expectation, but the overlap, to be modern. At least for a while to come, one should be on the lookout everywhere, and stubbornly disciplined about it.

Stated differently: One should learn to be an expert in apprenticeship *(4)*, because the modern subject is constantly different *(5)*.

Footnotes

(1) Jorge Luis Borges, *The Analytical Language of John Wilkins*: "… animals are divided into (a) those that belong to the Emperor, (b) embalmed ones, (c) those that are trained, (d) suckling pigs, (e) mermaids, (f) fabulous ones, (g) stray dogs, (h) those that are included in this classification, (i) those that tremble as if they were mad, (j) innumerable ones, (k) those drawn with a fine camel's hair brush, (l) others, (m) those that have just broken a flower vase, (n) those that resemble flies from a distance." One is led to wonder about the influence of language (labels) on specialization, and how expertise has formed (and might still change) according to our arbitrary nomenclature.

(2) Borges again, *Dreamtigers*: a passage that describes the author's lifelong passion for *the tiger*, so great that even in his sleep and dreaming, he seeks to cause this excellent majestic creature to appear. When sometimes the animal does show up, it is "stuffed or flimsy, or with impure variations of shape, or of an implausible size, or all too fleeting, or with a touch of the dog or the bird [about it]." Those who have attempted to start a business may get the lifelike realism of this fantastic vision best.

(3) Arthur Rimbaud, poet, merchant, and traveler in pursuit of many ventures: He met his end in the desert of Abyssinia; providing further proof, if this was necessary, that place, time, conditions, interaction, traffic, learning, are all as

important to enterprise and creative success as are more individual traits such as inspiration and energy. Rimbaud's art was a product of Paris, as much as it was of Rimbaud.

(4) "I'll know my song well before I start singing…" According to *Chronicles, Volume One*, it did not occur to Bob Dylan to write original songs until he had practiced and accumulated a repertory of many hundreds of covers. Among his earliest originals, subsequently, there is the quoted line.

(5) Patti Smith, circa 1979: "This is the era where everybody creates," a modular ad lib within her cover of an older hit: *So You Want To Be A Rock'n'Roll Star*. I remember with nostalgia the poker game that I programmed in BASIC at around that same time; it had to be printed out (the program itself, and the game's inputs and outputs) on perforated paper for the teacher to grade. (I don't recall the specifics of that, but have my suspicions.)

D. Ramsden

Tools for a new trade

About the author

Dan Ramsden has been professionally active in institutional capital markets and investment banking for more than twenty years. In the past decade his focus has turned exclusively to the digital sectors and their innovations, some early impressions of which are collected in a previous publication, *The Age of Convergence*. The author's current interests run most deeply to the value of networks, a recurring theme throughout the present volume.

The author's experience has taught him certain fundamental precepts, one of which is this: Everything changes, many things relate, and some things repeat. Knowing which of these things is which is the ongoing challenge in technology, commerce, and finance, which are all connected.

Outside of his commercial endeavors, the author teaches a course on private equity at Fordham University, incorporating many of the ideas contained herein.

www.ingramcontent.com/pod-product-compliance
Lightning Source LLC
Chambersburg PA
CBHW060348190526
45169CB00002B/521